Hooks 101:

How to Make $99 an Hour

By Terran Marks

Table of Contents

Why Hooks?   4

Shop Setup   6

Necessary Tools   8

So, What About That $99 An Hour?   12

A Hook From Start to Finish   15

Just the Basics, Please.   24

Other Blacksmithing Books   27

About the Author   28

Why Hooks?

Hooks may seem a little mundane to write an entire book about. You might be wondering why this book isn't about fire tools or ornamental iron gates or making animal heads out of steel.

The reason none of those projects are featured in this book is that hooks are one of the things that sell most often. Throughout your career as a blacksmith you will sell some gates, knives, fire tools, and animal heads if you choose to focus on those things. But I can guarantee that you will do much more business with your regular, everyday items.

In this book, we'll be focusing on a simple design that you can use to sell hundreds of hooks. Hooks and other household items will be your bread and butter goods.

Alright! With that out of the way, I'd like to introduce myself. My name is Terran Marks. I'm a blacksmith, firefighter, and writer.

I learned this trade at the John C. Campbell Folk School in North Carolina a few years ago and haven't stopped thinking about it since. Through trial and error, I've built a small blacksmithing business (Brown County Forge) and an Internet resource (The DIY Blacksmithing Site) used by thousands of smiths around the world every month.

I'm glad you decided to pick up this book. It's the second book in my Blacksmith Books Series and offers the next step toward becoming a self-sustaining blacksmith.

In it you'll find a step-by-step guide to creating one of the most purchased forged items. We will cover shop setup, tool selection and creation, shaping techniques, quenching, and finishing. By the end of it you will have a detailed plan for getting started.

Speaking of getting started, let's get going!

Shop Setup

To get to that $99/hour takes a little bit of advance planning. This first part may be a little dry, but bear with me. It's worth the few minutes of fine-tuning before you get started.

First, consider the workflow diagram below.

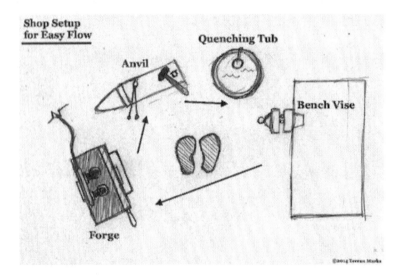

If you follow the arrows, you'll see how the movement works. Everything in the shop is within reach from the standing position in the center.

Your steel blanks move from the bench to the forge. Once they're at forging temperature, they move to the anvil. Then they go from the anvil to the quenching tub and bench vise. Then it's back to the forge.

With this setup or one similar, you shouldn't have to take more than a single step to get to anything. When you're all set, let's move on to the necessary tools for the job.

Necessary Tools

Just as you wouldn't go up on your roof to lay down shingles without a nail gun or hammer and nail pouch, you wouldn't try to forge a hook without these 7 things.

- Hammer

- Tongs

- U Bar – This neat little tool will get your hook bends nice and tight. It's easy to make, too. Just take 10 inches of ½" round bar stock (1018 mild steel will do) and spend a little time bending it into a narrow "U" shape. After you're done, cut off any excess material and use a metal file or belt sander to smooth the ends. Use mine for reference:

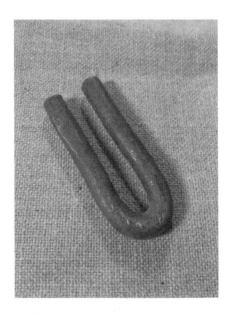

- Bench vise or post vise – I went down to the hardware store to get one similar to this one. You'll be clamping your U-bar in the vise during setup.

- Quenching Tub – It doesn't have to be a huge oil drum. I've used an empty soup can effectively for this project. We're only going to quench a small part of the hook anyway.

- Forge

- Anvil

Now that you have everything gathered together and put in its proper place, let's talk briefly about the materials I like to use.

Materials

You could use high carbon tool steel to make your wall hooks, but it would be overkill. 1018 mild steel, like you used to make the U-bar, works just fine. The thing to remember is to let it cool on its own. **Don't quench it**.

If you quench it, you'll cool it so fast that it becomes brittle. It may not fail immediately, but over time and with added weight it could break.

This may not be a big deal for your personal use, but imagine selling a set of hooks to someone and getting that email or phone call telling you that your carefully crafted hooks broke.

It's better to exercise some patience and set them aside while you work on other things. In this case, **more hooks**!

Round, Square, or Flat?

I prefer to use flat stock for my hooks for two reasons:

1. Flat stock is smooth and shows the hammer strokes.

2. It's easy to work and doesn't require flattening. For example, the round bar in the following photo had to be flattened at the top to hang properly.

Sizing

I've made various sizes of hooks, but the standard for me starts out as a piece of ¾" wide, 1/8" thick flat bar. I cut it into 5" long blanks with a horizontal band saw, hacksaw, or have a steel supplier make the cuts for me for a small fee ahead of time and file or sand down the edges (this gives it a smoother finished look).

In the next section, we'll finally get back to the question of the day: What about that $99/hour?

Thanks for sticking with me!

So, What About That $99 An Hour?

When I was first starting out as a blacksmith, I was told repeatedly that "Hooks are your bread and butter." It didn't hit home until I tried to sell some of my other hand-forged items alongside the hooks. Guess what sold.

The hooks.

The hooks always sell. You can forge the most beautiful fire poker, take professional grade photos of it, and post it to your website or Etsy. Nine times out of ten you're going to sell that set of three hooks first.

How did I end up making $99/hour making and selling hooks? I did it with these 5 things in mind.

1. Efficiency

2. Simple design

3. Competitive and reasonable pricing

4. Great photos

5. Clear writing

Let's go deeper into each of these.

Efficiency

This goes back to the shop setup I wrote about earlier. Having everything in its proper place saves a lot of time. This is invaluable when you move from forging a single hook in 30 minutes to 9 hooks and hour.

Simple Design

No added fanciness. You're not creating jewelry here. You're making a durable, rustic hook suitable for cabins, Arts and Crafts-style homes, and shabby-chic houses.

Competitive and Reasonable Pricing

I started out charging $11 per hook to factor in my time and effort, but I'm also careful to stay competitive in the market. If everyone else is charging $20 per hook, mine might be seen as cheap.

You have to find the sweet spot between self-compensation and providing value to your customers.

Great Photos

It's much easier to sell something with a visual aid. Before the Internet came along people interacted face-to-face with blacksmiths more often. They could hold the hooks in their hands and watch the smith do the work.

Now that the Internet is here, the focus is on detailed, well-lit photos. You have to be able to convey the texture and size of the hooks without the ability to put them in the customer's hands.

Clear Writing

You might be able to get away with just great photos. It's more likely that your descriptions and the stories you tell about your pieces will make the difference.

This is where you talk about the size of the item, how you made it, and any special features and uses. Writing clearly with great photos will keep hooks moving out your door and into people's homes.

And the $99?

Take the number of hooks you can make in an hour (9 is a good average) and multiply by the price per hook ($11). That's the $99/hour.

Now let's get into the creation of a hook from start to finish!

A Hook From
Start to Finish

To create my larger hooks I use 1/8" thick, 3/4" wide
flat bar stock.

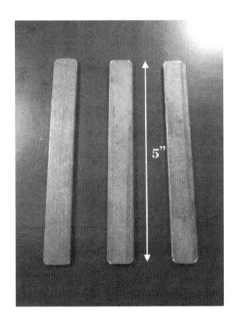

I cut 5" pieces from a longer length of flat bar stock
using a hacksaw. If you have access to a band saw
this will go a lot faster. Especially with a horizontal
band saw (one of the coolest cutting machines in
history).

*Note: Switching out the band for one suitable for
cutting metal rather than wood will reduce the risk of
snapped bands and make your work much easier.*

I prefer to start with smooth edges, so after I cut my mild steel blanks (1018 mild steel is a good choice) from my bar stock, I file down the edges like you see in the photo. You'll see the nicer looking finish it gives the hook later in the book.

You want to start with a piece of steel that's longer than the finished hook you're planning to make. The reason for this is the loss of length that will occur when you curve one end around to form the bend of the hook.

Firing Up the Forge (and what to do while it gets hot)

So, you have your blanks cut and ready. To save a little time, you'll fire up the forge while you file down the edges.

You can also get your U-bar securely clamped in your vise. This is where you'll be doing your hook bending.

Note: The U-bar isn't hardened in any special way as you might expect with a forged tool. The amount of heat the U-bar sustains doesn't require any special treatment.

Forging Temperature

I'm assuming you're using a gas forge for this tutorial. Doing this process with a coal forge is straightforward. It just requires a little more attention while the metal heats up. You don't want your metal to get too hot.

The benefit of a gas forge is that you don't have to worry about things overheating. Adjust your gas flow with the regulator at the beginning, monitor the color of your first few hooks, and make a note of that dial setting.

You want your steel blanks to get to yellow-orange (about 1700 degrees Fahrenheit, 927 centigrade) before pulling them out to start work. Pulling them out sooner will make it take longer, believe it or not.

The first thing you're going to do is bring your first blank to the anvil with your tongs in your non-dominant hand. This is where you're going to flatten the ends. It's an optional step, but it shows off your hammer strokes in all the right places. It also adds a little style to an otherwise boring piece of bent metal.

If you can't get both ends flattened in one heat, put the blank back in and grab another one. Flatten it and repeat.

When you have both ends flattened, take the glowing yellow-orange piece of metal to the anvil. Now you're going to put that little curve on the working end of the hook. Use the close-up below for reference.

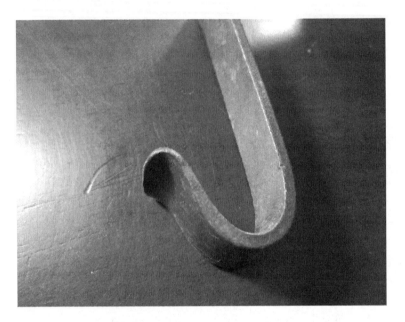

See the delicate curve on the end? That keeps the hook from catching on garments, handbags, etc.

To make that curve, use the edge of the anvil and place just the tip over it. Gently hammer it over the edge until you're satisfied with your curve.

If you've lost your heat, put it back in the forge and grab another flat-ended blank and repeat.

If you can do it in one heat, take the flattened blank with the curved tip to the quenching tub. **Remember, you're not going to submerge the hook.** You just want to cool the tip so you can bend the blank around your U-bar. If you didn't quench and instantly harden the curved tip, you would end up bending it back and reversing the work you just did.

Take your time when you're getting the hang of it. The saying "slow is smooth, smooth is fast" applies here. If you need to do it in a few more heats, do it that way.

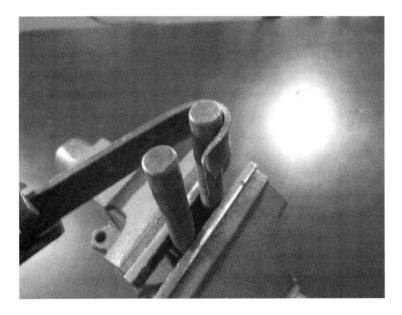

When you're satisfied with your bend, put the hook (yep, it is now officially a hook) back into the forge and repeat until you have your set of three or five. I like to work in sets of five so a hook is always going into the forge as one if coming out.

The reason the hook goes back into the forge is so you can correct any unwanted bends and scrape off all that scale. You want it to be as smooth as possible before drilling and finishing.

Drilling and Finishing

Once the hook is free of scale and as close to perfect as we want it, we will set it aside on some bricks to cool. Why bricks? They allow for slower cooling than a metal bench top and leave a nice reddish patina on the hook.

It's personal preference mostly, but you definitely don't want to quench it. Rapid cooling like that will leave it brittle. Just set it aside while you work on other things.

Once the cooling is done, take a center punch or prick punch and a hammer (**not** your blacksmithing hammer) and place a small divot near the top of the hook to guide the drill bit.

I've drilled the holes for hooks with a hand drill and a drill press. I prefer the drill press. It's easier on the elbows and it provides more leverage and power.

It's good to have the size of hardware you want to use in mind before you drill the holes. I use #6 and #8 wood screws most of the time so a 1/8, 9/64, or 5/32 bit does the job.

Finishing

After drilling, you might have some burrs around your mounting holes. Use a file or a belt sander to get rid of these.

Now it's time to decide one what type of finish you're going to use on your hooks. I focus on traditional techniques as much as possible and prefer a natural beeswax finish.

This is achieved by briefly reheating the hook with a torch and rubbing a piece of beeswax on it. Be careful not to get the metal so hot that it produces flames. The finish won't be as good and you'll have to wait for it to cool a little.

To do this type of finish, you'll need these supplies:

- Your hook
- A small propane canister (14.1 oz./400g) and a nozzle
- Beeswax
- Tongs
- Flint striker

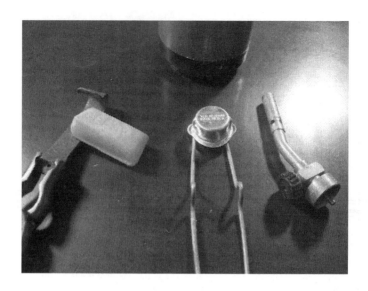

(Finishing supplies.)

Here are the steps to follow once you have your supplies together:

Light the propane torch.*

Holding the hook with the tongs and the torch in your other hand, move the flame slowly across the surface of the hook for at least 10 seconds (this isn't a strict number).

Set the torch down in a safe place or turn it off.

Rub the beeswax across the hook's surface. If it's melting, we're good. Coat the whole hook.

Wipe off the excess wax and set the still hot hook aside.

Repeat with your other hooks.

*The heating portion can also be done with your forge. Just keep an eye on how long you leave your hooks in there. They should still be gray and not hot enough to flame up when you put the wax on them.

You can also use paint to finish your hooks. Krylon or Rustoleum in colored finishes or clear coats do a fine job. You just have to decide if you want to cover up your work in that way.

That's it!

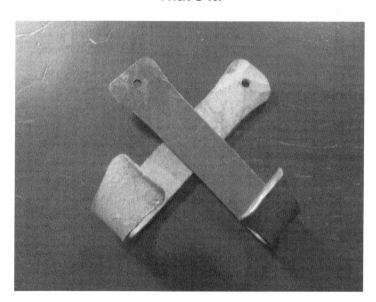

A Handy Cheat Sheet

If that's all making sense and you'd like a quick reference guide, the next two pages can be hung in your shop and used by themselves.

Just the Basics, Please.

Here's what I do, in 12 steps, to forge 9 hooks an hour that sell for $11 per hook.

1. The forge is lit first thing to get it up to temperature while I set everything else up.

2. I clamp my U-bar in the post vise making sure it's not going anywhere. This is where I bend the hooks.

3. I lay my hammer and tongs on the anvil. Hammer by my right hand. Tongs at my left. Switch this if you're a lefty.

4. The quenching tub is between the anvil and post vise. This allows me to move smoothly between the anvil and post vise, doing localized quenching as I go.

5. I put five pre-cut flat bar blanks with filed edges into the forge and close the door.

6. Once they're up to a nice yellow-orange, I pull one out and flatten both ends.

7. Back in it goes and out comes another.

8. Repeat until all of the blanks have flattened ends.

9. In the next pass, I lightly curve one flattened end over the smooth side of the anvil, quench just the

tip, then hammer the bend around the U-bar. It goes back into the forge and I repeat until all five hooks are done.

10. I take the first hook out and, using a wire brush, scrape away the scale (loose metal that flakes off while forging) and correct any bending where I don't want it.

11. Repeat. As I pull one hook out to cool on bricks, I put another blank into the forge to heat while I work.

12. I briefly reheat each hook with a propane torch and coat them in beeswax. Wiping off the beeswax, I set them aside to cool completely.

And that's one way to make $99 an hour!

Can I ask a favor?

Thanks for picking up **Hooks 101: How to Make $99 an Hour**! Hopefully, you now have some inspiration and actionable steps to take to start forging.

If this book was helpful to you, I would really appreciate you leaving a review on Amazon. By leaving an honest review you make it easier for aspiring blacksmiths to find good information. Help spread the word!

Other Blacksmithing Books

The DIY Blacksmithing Book

U.S. Blacksmith Schools: Find a Blacksmithing Class Near You

2017 Anvil and Forge Buying Guide

About the Author

Terran Marks is a firefighter, blacksmith, and writer who, like Vulcan, spends most of his time working with a silent intensity. He makes his online home at the **DIY Blacksmithing Site** and can be found working in his shop **Brown County Forge**.

You can connect with Terran on the DIY Blacksmithing Facebook page, Brown County Forge's Facebook page, or send him an email at diyblacksmith@gmail.com.

Helpful links:

facebook.com/diyblacksmithing

facebook.com/browncountyforge

browncountyforge.com

diyblacksmith.blogspot.com

Made in the USA
Lexington, KY
01 September 2019